Magickal Herbal

Teas & Incense

Recipes

By

Taren S

ISBN: 9798846738720
Imprint: Independently published

DEDICATION

To all my YouTube folks- crossroads Witches and other interesting magickal beings.

CONTENTS

Part 1

DEFINITION & USES OF MAGICKAL HERBS

What is considered an "Herb"?
In Herbal magick, a "herb" considered any plant that is useful to humans. This includes fruits, vegetables, flowers, trees, shrubs, grasses, and weeds. Generally, any plant that can be used for cooking, medicine, fragrance, clothing, or we can make useful objects from it.

Also, keep in mind that this definition of "herb" applies to plants that have physical benefits to the body, as well as to those that are known to be baneful and potentially deadly (such as belladonna and henbane). For those who have a developed a deep understanding and connection to herbs magickally, know that no plant is good or bad. But each has its own distinct uses.

Herbs can be used to cure or to curse, as well as to conjure or to banish spirits, lesser deities, and entities. They can enchant our gardens and our homes. They can help guide us on the path to transformation and self-improvement. But, most importantly, herbal magick can open the door to spiritual realms and other worlds; serve to connect a human being with Mother Nature and the Divine.

Magickal Herbs

There probably exists no plant or tree that has not at one time, in some part of the world, been used in a working (spell) or potion or utilized as an amulet. And it is said that all parts of a plant, whether they be roots, buds, flowers, stems, or bark, are magickally significant.

Historically, belief in the magickal properties of plants was by no means restricted only to Pagans and pre-Christian religions. Numerous references to herbal magick and botanomancy (the art and practice of divination by plants) can be found throughout the Bible, from the burning bush oracle of Moses to Rachel's use of mandrake roots to magickally increase her fertility, to Jacob's magickal use of striped poplar, almond, and plane-tree rods to bring forth striped, speckled, and spotted livestock offspring.

In contemporary times, as it has been in the past, herbal magick remains an essential part of the Witches' craft. It can be used to assist an individual in attracting a compatible lover, landing the right job, changing bad luck into good, and even increasing one's wealth! Empowered by the energies of elements, elementals and a Divine source, herbs have long been used as amulets to protect against evil, dried and burned as magickal incense during rituals, and added to cauldron brews.

Whether you are trying to fine tune your intuition or tap into your inherent extrasensory perception abilities, creating a peaceful workspace externally is just as essential as your internal peace. In today's hectic fast paced world, it may be hard to find your inner calm. Good health and practice can also be aided by oils, herbs, and incense to help unlock your natural psychic abilities, and better attune yourself to Divinity and the world around you.

Herbs are derived from plants that have a specific vibrational frequency or spiritual connection. These powerful vibrations and connections can help in energizing, balancing, and cleansing your chakras, auras, and other internal energy flows. The various components of these herbs interact with our body's energy system and remove accumulated toxins, improve blood circulation, and enhance the oxygen flow.

The herbs also affect our psyche through the detoxification process and help us ground as well as connect to the higher consciousness and realms. Using specific herbs that resonate with a chakra or energic flow will help you achieve a balanced state of mind, spirit, and body.

Scientific Relevance of Herbs in Healing

A paper published in 2011 highlighted various therapeutic, antioxidant and antibacterial properties of Holy Basil, which help with better physical and mental wellbeing. In another study, the calming aroma of Lavender and Rosemary have been proven to aid in uplifting the mood and cognitive performance in healthy adults. A review on the scientific basis of the use of Ashwagandha found 'encouraging results' of ashwagandha's therapeutic uses with little to no toxicity.

Hence it is quite safe to say that imbibing herbs in our daily routine will definitely affect chakra functioning or internal energic flows. Even though many researchers have found positive effects of herbs on our physical and mental well-being, you should always consult an expert before you start consuming them.

Herbal magick is a tradition that dates to antiquity when medicine was not separated from magick and has been used for many purposes. It has been practiced by healers, root workers, shamans, cunning folk, and of course, folkloric, or traditional Witches all over the world.

Physical healing was often supplemented by ritual and prayer. The patient could be treated with an herbal tea infusion as well as a smudging ritual and an incantation to the spirits for a quick recovery. In addition to healing, plants were used to magickal works, such as the creation of potions, talismans, amulets, and spells.

Plants are living entities that possess their own energy and properties. And it is wise to remember we work with the plant; they are our allies. We do not use them. The combination of healing and magickal properties makes herbs powerful components in modern magick.

Herbal magick is a type of natural magick. This means that:
Incorporates all four elements.
It does not need a lot of preparation and tools to perform.
You can practice it anywhere, using what you have right underneath your feet. Look in your yard, take a walk in nature.

The Elemental Balance of Plants
In terms of magickal meaning, plants personify the power of the four elements that interact to develop and sustain life. They start as seeds on the Earth's soil, where the minerals required to maintain their life are located.

They engage with the "fire" of sunlight, that makes the procedure of transforming co2 into oxygen feasible (a process that has a direct effect on air quality). Air, subsequently, promotes more plant life in the form of wind. It strengthens the growth of stems and leaves and spreads seeds to continue the cycle.

Without stating the obvious, all plants need water to live and grow. However, they play an essential role in Earth's water cycles by cleansing water and assisting to move it from the ground to the atmosphere. There is no better example of how the elements of Earth, Air, Water, and Fire collaborated than in the magickal existence of plants.

Herbs are Mother Nature's gifts to all of humankind, regardless of spiritual beliefs, magickal tradition, or culture. And whether you pride yourself as a country Witch or an urban magick folk, herbs can reward you with a wealth of enchantment, divination, and folklore.

Advice on Usage of Magickal Herbs

Once you have acquired your supply of herbs, a few suggestions regarding storage. Herbs are best kept in a cool, dry, dark location to maximize their lifespan. Excessive heat and moisture can cause them to become moldy, and prolonged strong sunlight can dry out and fade them. Specific methods of storage are up to you.

Keep them in their plastic bags, stored in a cabinet. Transfer them to attractive glass jars with fun labels and fancy ornamental stoppers. Whatever makes you feel magickal and keeps your herbs fresh and easily accessible is the goal. I would recommend that you keep herbs only for around a year or less depending on the herb. Some have a longer shelf life than others. Doing this will ensure that you are using fresh, vibrant herbs for your magickal and spiritual workings.

And now, dear crossroad Witches and other interesting magickal beings; a note on safe usage. PLEASE ask your doctor if it's safe for you to ingest any herb if you have any concerns! If you can't be certain of an herb's toxicity – or lack thereof – it's best to err on the side of caution and refrain from ingesting it in any way.

Part 2

TEAS IN HISTORY

Brief History of Tea

Tea is a beverage with a very long history – probably the longest in human race. Legend has it, that the Chinese emperor Shen-nong discovered the herb in 2737 BC as the leaves accidentally fallen into the hot water he was drinking. Thus, amazed by tea magick, the emperor dedicated his life to the invention of tea brews and the magick the comes out of each. Since then, the lines between medicinal use and magickal/folklore have blended.

In Tibet, tea-drinkers would receive barley wine as well. They would dip their finger in the wine and then flick it away three times before drinking the tea. This symbol of restraint served as an offering to Buddha, Sangha, and Dharma.

Ancient Egyptian papyri, including the Ebers papyrus, listed the medicinal uses of herbs in tea. These doctors were usually priests who believed that spirits blocked channels in the human body. They accompanied herbal medicinal tea with rituals to heal their patients.

Drinking tea alone is a form of meditation. Drinking tea with others is a form of community. Taking the time to prepare tea is an act of caring for yourself or another. When we give tea the time and care in deserves, it returns to us all its infinite gifts.

The most powerful health benefit of tea is completely overlooked by modern science: tea asks of us a few moments out of our day to prepare and appreciate it. This means that we are forced by our daily ritual to relax and recover, forced to take time to think about what we have achieved and what we wish to achieve. Twenty minutes of daily relaxation is just as critical to our physical health as twenty minutes of daily exercise if it manages to keep our stress levels in check.

Magickal tea use can be categorized into three uses: divination, offering, and workings support." I will explain the last term when I get there.

Tea Divination

You've probably heard about tea leaf reading before. Also called tasseography, the practice tells your fortune through wine sediments, coffee grounds, or of course, tea leaves. Tea leaf divination first appeared in Scotland and the United Kingdom after the Dutch brought tea from China.

In the Encyclopedia of Occultism & Parapsychology, J. Gordon Melton details that the diviner pours the tea without using a strainer. Whoever's fortune needs to be told will drink the tea, but not all of it. After swirling the cup around, the diviner will read the shapes in the tea leaves. This is either done through a fortune telling cup or, traditionally, by reading the shapes from the outside in. The outer rim depicts the near future, while the middle illustrates the far future.

Offerings

In my opinion, tea is one of the best drinks to use as an offering. It is highly customizable, and I've found that certain deities and spirits enjoy different teas. However, don't be surprised if an entity doesn't accept tea and prefers a glass of wine. You may want to consider your offering tea based on the folklore and correspondences that are associated with that aspect/Deity/Entity.

Working Support

"Working support" is a term to describe using tea in a magickal environment/setting. In essence, the tea itself is not the actual working. But when you combine it with ritual or to set a magickal energy, it will produce results. Hence, the tea acts more like a working tool than a working within itself.

So how do you transform regular tea into magickal tea that produces results? By connecting to and activating each ingredient used. The Spirit of the Herb is already there, you just need to connect and activate (infuse them with your energy) them. Then they lend you power for your magickal mystical endeavors.

How To Brew a Herbal Tea

Boil Water - The goal here is to boil the water so that it's so hot that it quickly and easily infuses into the herbs and works to pull out the properties of the herbs.

Place Tea In Strainer - There are a lot of options. I personally like using loose leaf herbs with a ball strainer but if your making tea for more than one person you may wish to use a loose-leaf teapot which has a strainer compartment built in.

Pour Hot Water - Simply pour the water in the tea pot or into the cup with your strainer in.

Steep Your Herbs - Steep times will vary depending upon what herb you're using and how hard (or tough) it is. For most leaves and flowers, 10 minutes of steeping is perfect.

How To Make a Herbal Infusion

An herbal infusion is what most folks refer to as "tea".

Place required amount of herb in warmed China or glass teapot or cafetière (but nothing metal), 1 oz (26g) of dried herb.

Pour boiling water in 1 pint (500ml).

Leave it to infuse for approx 10 minutes.

Strain through a sieve.

How To Make a Herbal Decoction

You need to make a decoction if using woody/dense herbs, roots, or barks. Crush up plant components with a pestle and mortar.

Pour 1 oz (25 g) of ground dried plants matter in a stainless steel, glass or ceramic saucepan.

Add 1 ½ pints (750 ml) of cold water to saucepan.

Bring to boil, reduce heat and allow to simmer for approx. 1 hour (the volume should reduce by about a third).

Strain and add water to make up the required amount.

All teas can be refrigerated for up to 48 hours.

Complete Magickal Tea Full Moon Ritual

Tea brewing involves the union of the five alchemical elements. This is what can make a tea ritual a powerful kind of natural magick. You don't even need a magickal circle for it to work (you can still cast one to help you, though!).

Elemental Correspondences

Earth: The herbs in your tea

Air: The steam and scent of your tea

Fire: The warmth needed for tea brewing

Water: The medium of your tea, its liquid state.

Aether/Spirit: Since aether is made from the combination of the four other elements, by drinking tea, you are creating and honoring aether.

First, acquire your ingredients and understand why you are using each one. Grab a sachet or tea strainer to put the ingredients in. Before you place it in, hold it, and infuse it with energy. There are several ways to do this. One is to chant; repeat your intention over and over, and don't be afraid to whisper, yell, or laugh.

You can also charge each herb one by one by passing your hands through them. Imagine that a white light goes from your hands to the herbs. When you feel the herbs tingling with energy, put them into your teapot or tea bag.

You may also breath out 3 times before releasing a long, slow, deep breath onto the ingredient. This is called a magickal breath. Do this with each ingredient before steeping. As the tea steeps, continue. Talk into it. Dance around.

The key is to make it mindfully, with intention. Be conscious of how you feel and try to stay in the moment. Remember that the steps of the following ritual are only guidelines. I encourage you to customize it to what you like, according to your own culture and traditions.

Heat the water in your kettle. While you are waiting for the water to boil, prepare yourself and your sacred space. Ground yourself. Burn some incense. Light a candle. Play your favorite music.

When it is ready, pour the hot water on the herbs. Focus on what you are doing. This is the activation phase: you really need to be focused while doing it. Imagine that the hot water activates the magickal properties of the plants. If it helps you, visualize that the plants' auras are changing color, from white to purple.

Find a place where you can see the moon. Sit near a window, or if the weather allows it, go outside.
Important: do not drink your tea right away. Breathe in the aroma, take a deep breath while visualizing your intention. Sip your tea and let the energy of the Full moon fill your insides.

This is a loving, healing, protective energy. Breathe it. Bathe in it. Immerse yourself in it. Give yourself over to it. Imagine that it merges into your aura, filling your soul. Again, say out loud your intention.

When there is only a small sip of tea left, stop drinking. Pour the last drop of tea into the ground as an offering. Thank the Full Moon and the Universe for their help. Above all, thank yourself.
Write what you have felt in your journal.

Part 3

HERBS USED IN TEA TRECIPES

Tea Bases Used
Green Tea
Rooisbos Tea
Black Tea
White Wine
Red Wine
Rum clear
Lemon-Lime Soda

Herbs Used
*denotes a Health Warning

Apple
dried/slice- numerous health benefits

Ashwagandha*
Lowers blood sugar. an adaptogen herb that natural action is to balance, especially the thyroid. It is nutritive and calming. Magickally, it increases your strength and stamina and increases sexual prowess.

Bay Leaf

a favorite for prophesy by the priestesses of the Oracle of Delphi. This herb brings good loving and protects from evil

Blueberries

dried- high in antioxidants. A representation of the lapis lazuli necklace given up by Innana in her descent.

Calendula*

do not use if pregnant or breast feeding. Otherwise known as Marigold, it is a visionary solar plant. It aids in divination and are little sparks of light. They heal and soothe inflamed skin as well as the digestive tract.

Caraway Seeds

relaxes digestive tract. These seeds protect from theft of mate or item. They attract energies that want to be committed.

Cardamon Pods*

can trigger gall stones. It warms, stimulates, and uplifts the mind. It brings clarity with openness.

Chamomile*

can cause an allergic reaction. These flowers are little suns that act as guardians to any space. They are calming and protective, while purifying.

Cinnamon

stick/powder- Helps with digestive complaints. In magick, acts as a power punch and energy vibration booster. It stimulates psychic power and focuses the mind for better communication.

Clover

white or red-traditionally used for respiratory ailments. It is also soothing to the skin. Its two main magickal uses are for money and love, especially fidelity.

Damiana*

lowers blood sugar. This has very similar actions magickally and physically, that is as an aphrodisiac. It increases your magickal and psychic ability. It is also touted as an anti-depressant and nerve tonic.

Dandelion leaves

this is a great diuretic because the leaves are filled with potassium. It has a positive action on the kidneys and the renal system. It is tied to divination and wish granting and calling out to spirits.

Echinacea

helps immunity system. It is a higher realm herb. It strengthens the magickal power of all workings used in.

Elderberries

dried-promotes healthy immune system and soothes a scratchy throat. These are the berries of the Elder Mother and they bring her mysteries.

Feverfew*

Do not use during pregnancy. It wards and protects against disease. It is often used for headaches, respiratory ailments, and nervous conditions.

Ginger

root/powder-a great nausea remedy. Magickally it is a cool, bright punch of power. It increases confidence and has attractive properties.

Ginkgo Biloba*

Do not ingest if you are on blood thinners. Gingko Biloba is the leaf of a magickal ancient tree that almost died out but was saved and brought back by monks. It increases the blood flow in your brain and your magick along with it.

Ginseng

powder-good for mental health and general vitality. Siberian Ginseng, or

Eleuthero, is strongly masculine. Panax Ginseng is a tonic to the body where American Panax quinquefolius, or American Ginseng is a yin tonic.

Goat's Rue*

powder-might lower blood sugar levels. It is a deeply healing herb.

Hawthorn Berries

antioxidant. A heart strengthener and tonic. It is used to draw love to you or shine heart chakra energy.

Helichrysum

promotes energy, beauty, and longevity. At one time it was a panacea for all sorts of medical issues. Today, it is used to calm mental strife.

Hibiscus

lowers body temperature. Use in any summer working or where passion and love are desired.

Honey*

do not give to infants under 1 year old. Honey has attractive, sticky properties, physically and magickally. Bees and honey are sacred to Artemis. It is used for its purification properties. It never goes bad.

Hyssop

digestive aid. Used for respiratory ailments. Magickally it is an herb of purification. It is a ritual herb mentioned in the Psalms.

Lavender

calming agent. Connected to the third eye, it is a higher realm herb that will increase the vibration of all around.

Lemon

numerous health benefits. It is especially sacred to Diana.

Lemon Balm

soothing properties. It is also called Melissa. It brings love and friendship and heals a broken heart. It is an herb of joy, treating depression and anxiety among its many physical properties.

Lemon Grass

It is gently stimulating to the nervous system and aids in digestion. It is used in Magick for strength, courage, and honesty. It is about standing firm to what you believe. It is also tied to divination.

Lemon Verbena

eases digestion. It ousts negativity and replaces it nicely. It is an herb to use when you want to get rid of the old and bring in the new.

Marshmallow Root

soothing agents, a demulcent. It soothes the throat and really the entire digestive tract, and gently opens the throat chakra.

Meadowsweet

Its main component is salicylic acid, also found in aspirin. It brings a happy lovely energy, full of buoyancy and expectancy.

Mint

fresh/sprig- freshens breath and aids in digestion. This is a powerful, ambitious, and lucky herb. Its power lies in its hardiness. Once you plant mint, you will never get rid of it. It gives a mild punch of magickal power.

Mugwort*

do not take in any amount if pregnant or breast feeding. Mugwort is used for divination and prophesy. It is a darker herb and believed to invoke Hecate. Also known as wormwood, it has been used as a pain remedy and a killer of free radicals.

Mullein

Mainly used in respiratory remedies. Mullein is important as a springtime herb. It is also a guard against malevolence.

Nettle

nourishes the whole body. Great for the skin and conditions of too much blood. It is magickally used for healing, purification, and for uncrossing.

Nutmeg

good for the heart and the entire circulatory system. Acts in a beneficial way to boost brain power. This is an ancient spice that willing to give its good luck to those who ask. Its sweet smell is associated with the divine feminine.

Oat Straw

nourishes the whole body. This herb is all about strength. Strength of back, strength of will, strength of courage. It has a wild shadow as an aphrodisiac.

Orris Root

powder-blood purifier and favorite to Marie Laveau. It stimulates the appetite and bile production. It is a root that draws love and is associate with the moon and purification.

Pansy flower

many health benefits, they bring love and happiness.

Passionflower

promotes positive mental state. It both calms heated angry passions and incites love passions

Plantain

acts as a drawing agent to the skin. Has many health benefits. It has protection qualities and combats weariness. It magickally aids the head and all women's womb issues.

Red Peppers*

dried- do not take if have digestive issues, numerous health benefits. A power punch of the strongest variety, they encourage free movement of energy especially through the heart. Can also be used to play tricks on person, cross, or jinx.

Rose Petals

numerous skin benefits. Rose petals can be used to draw benefits based upon the color of the flower. Generally, Red for passionate love, Pink for love or friendship, yellow for friendship, white for purification, etc.

Rosemary*

fresh/dried-avoid if pregnant, numerous health benefits. Use magickally for protection, and cleansing, and love. It is often used to enhance memory

Saint John's Wort

This is an herb of Midsummer and of protection. It is rumored to be loved by the little folk. It grants happiness and clarity magickally and physically.

Slippery Elm*

do not take if pregnant, good for digestive tract and throat. It opens the throat chakra. Just as it coats the throat allowing the energy to slide, it also lets all sorts of other spiteful words, like gossip and slander, to slip right off you.

Sow Thistle

Wide variety of medical benefits. This herb is sacred to Cerridwen.

White Willow Bark

Its main physical property is as a pain killer. It is considered a moon herb and a binding herb. All parts of willow are used in protection.

Wormwood

See Mugwort

Yarrow

a Witch's and a warrior's herb. It was named for Achilles who was both bathed in it as a babe and used it to heal his fellow soldiers. It is anti-inflammatory and used for wound healing. It is also used for acne and to sweat a fever. Magickally, you can use it for all sorts of things from finding love to enhancing psychic powers.

Part 4

INCENSE IN HISTORY

Brief History of Incense

The word "incense" is derived from the Latin "incensare" meaning to sacrifice, burn. Herbs are materials commonly used as incense to produce a fragrant scent. Alone or in combination with essentials oils and plant resin.

Walking through your flower garden in the morning, just as the first rays of sun warm its colorful petals, will transport, and lift your mood. This is perhaps the first aromatherapy experience that captured humanity's imagination.

Incense is a substance you can burn to produce an aromatic scent. The use of incense dates back to ancient times and was particularly popular in the ancient Babylonian empire as well as in Greece and Egypt. To this day, people of many different cultures use incense for aromatherapy, meditation, religious ceremonies and even for simple aesthetic reasons. Incense is also used to counteract unpleasant odors or to repel insects. Since that beginning, the fragrant smoke of ancient fires has risen in rhythm with the sun, the moon, and the tides: the heartbeats of life on earth.

History tells us that Incense has been used as a sacrifice to both Goddesses and Gods, as a smudge to help drive away evil spirits, and as a tool to draw in good luck, love, and wealth. The ancient Egyptians and Jewish folk were but two such peoples who blended and produced high-quality Incense for ritual use. You can even find mention of such recipes in the Bible and other older texts for some of these wonderful fragrant incense blends.

When you burn dried herbs or resins, you'll need a heat tolerant vessel. Traditionally this is an abalone shell with a bit of sand in the bottom. You might also use a charcoal disc beneath the herbs to keep them smoking, especially in the case of resins.

The burning of sweet gums, resins, woods, and plants has taken hundreds of beautiful, diverse cultural forms, many of which persist today. Ancient Egyptians burned offerings to the sun god, Ra, on his daily trek across the heavens. Frequent references to the use of incense in the Old Testament suggest that the Jews have used it since very early times. Modern Hindus burn camphor and incense before the image of Krishna. The Greeks burned sweet incenses to make sacrifice and prayer more acceptable to the gods.

By the fourteenth century, it had become part of most of the established Christian rituals and is still used for such ceremonies as high mass, processions, and funerals. Modern pagan practices also involve highly developed ritual uses of incense. In Native American religion, sage, sweet grass, yerba santa, uva-ursi, cedar, and tobacco are burned ceremonially for purifying oneself and one's environment, for sending up prayers to the Great Spirit, and for connecting with one's spirit guides or helpers.

Incense makes use of many botanical products which cannot be liquefied or distilled into a perfume. Tree barks and saps, gums, resins, roots, flowers, fragrant leaves, and needles can be combined in myriad ways to create a rising, mood-enhancing bouquet of fragrant smoke. The botanical ingredients may be purchased, grown, or gathered from the wild.

Incense can take many forms, from simple, loose ingredients to be thrown on glowing coals to ornately shaped cones, cylinders, sticks, or coils. All are fun to make and enjoyable to use. All except loose incense consist of four basic ingredients: an aromatic substance or mixture, a burnable base, a bonding agent, and a liquid to change the bonding agent into a glue. Coloring agents can be added as well.

Blending Aroma Energies

Beyond aesthetics, lighting incense can help to create the sense of a safe, purposeful, ritual space. Lighting fine incense fills a room with aroma, which is a powerful conscious and subconscious activator. Incense enhances the flavor of tea by awakening the senses. It can provide a flavor counterpoint for tea.

In this way, incense can make a tea tasting instantly feel special. Taking the time to light a stick or coil of incense marks a moment in time as special and worth enjoying. This simple act can help you pay more attention to your tea and make the tea better in the process.

The religious and scholarly roots of herbal history make incense an indispensable complement to the modern magickal tea moment. Lighting incense is a reminder to enjoy time with purpose and mindfulness; something now we need these days more than ever.

Incense offers a connection to a meaningful personal ritual, an evocation of nature and a celebration of our connection to Divinity as we know it in that moment. If we take the time to set out our tea ware and bring out our herbal tea blends, incense helps us to make a mundane act a very powerful magickal activity of self-care among other things we can use the energy for.

Incense also marks time in a meaningful way. Incense as hourglass was one of its earliest uses. In this way, lighting incense marks and sets out a period of time devoted to study, practice or just being in the moment. When paired with tea, a stick or coil of incense marks the amount of time you want to spend savoring a tea with purpose and with mindfulness.

Beyond all of this, incense is also a historical connection to the past. Incense has been enjoyed for hundreds of generations, nearly unchanged. Lighting a stick of herbal incense today is the same experience that an devote Priest in an ancient temple would have had hundreds, if not thousands of years ago.

Finally, the practice of incense allows us to enjoy an expression of the environment outside of the tea. We love tea for its connection to place. It is joyful to find another connection in incense that so strongly evokes place through aroma. It can transport you to a forest, a mountain, or a garden in a moment.

How to Make a Smudge Stick

Trim your herbs to your desired size

Attach a long piece of twine to the bottom of your herb bundle and wrap it around as tightly as you can until you reach the top.

Once you reach the top, tie your twine securely and trim off any excess

Allow your smudge stick to dry for a minimum of 2 weeks

When it's time to burn as incense, light your smudge stick with a lighter or match

Frankincense and Myrrh

Frankincense and myrrh are best known around the world as two of the gifts of the Magi in the Bible. Even before the Bible was written, these herbs were found in magickal guides all over the Middle East, northern Africa, and Europe. They are two of the most versatile, powerful ingredients you can have in your herb cabinet for workings and rituals.

Frankincense is a strongly solar herb. This makes it a suitable offering for sun gods, like Apollo, Bast, or Obatala. In Yule rituals to celebrate the return of the sun, frankincense is an excellent celebratory offering. To use resins as offerings, bless and dedicate them to the deities for which they are intended.

Both frankincense and myrrh are excellent for spiritual cleansing. Place either frankincense, myrrh, or a mixture of both resins onto a burning coal in an incense burner, and wave it around your home with a feather or fan. Make sure the smoke touches all of the walls. As you do this, speak your intention out loud.

Say something like, "*This incense smoke cleanses all it touches. Nothing bad may linger here, only good is welcome.*"

It is also suitable for purifying a ritual space before any magickal undertaking or working.
Mix frankincense and myrrh with any herbs or roots to boost their magickal powers.
Burn frankincense incense before and during meditations to help open your third eye chakra.
Use myrrh is any rituals dealing with hexes or protection against psychic attacks.
Burn frankincense and myrrh cones for a relaxed and calm environment.

Frankincense and myrrh are two ingredients no home should be without. They are powerful spiritual cleansers, welcome offerings to many forms and aspects of Divinity, potent healers, and a wonderful way to attract the things you desire.

Part 5

Herbs For Incense Recipes

This list only includes herbs used in the listed recipes in this book. There are many many more herbs, volumes actually, that contains recipes for incense. Start simple and find the ones that resonate with you and your magickal spiritual practice. Ultimately, no one can tell you the "right incense" to put on your altar, connect with your ancestors or spirit guides, or enhance your personal connections.

Here are plants used as incense and why they are burnt. Try growing some of them on your own property.

Agrimony
The Agrimony will send the curse back to whoever tried to put it on you. Agrimony is an herb of protection and reversal magick. It is used to break jinxes, and to turn them back upon the sender. In Hoodoo, Agrimony is considered to be one of the best herbs for counteracting the Evil Eye, slander, and gossip.

Angelica
This is a very powerful protection herb that creates a barrier against negative energy. This herb can be scattered for purification, protection,

and uncrossing. You can also add it to incense to promote healing or to the bath to remove curses, hexes, or spells. Sprinkle around the outside perimeter of the home for protection as well. Plus, you can burn it to bring a lost love back to you. Also Called: Masterwort, Archangel, Garden Angel, Angelica Root.

Basil

Having been cultivated for over 5000 years, it's no surprise that basil is one of the world's preferred herbs. Burning a little amount of basil can go a long way. Its aroma can be described as herbal with slightly spicy undertones. A versatile herb, basil leaves can be used for love, protection, or to attract wealth. Burned in an incense with rose petals, basil helps to restore peace in a relationship. Add to exorcism and protection incenses.

Bay Laurel Leaf

The Bay Laurel Leaf was awarded to only the most eloquent and victorious – the noble few. In ancient Greece and Rome, crowns of Bay Laurel were awarded to those who had mastered a fine art or won an impressive military victory. Bay Laurel Leaf is a symbol of courage, talent, artistry, and most of all: victory.

The Laurel was the tree of Apollo: Greek god of the Sun, wisdom, and creativity.   Bay Leaves were used by the Oracles at Delphi: the leaves were cast into a fire; if they crackled, the omen was good. If they did not, the omen was bad. Recipients of a good omen were awarded a crown of Laurels.   For this reason, laurel leaves are said to aid in divination, and to produce prophetic dreams. Due to their evergreen nature, laurel leaves are also a symbol of wealth.

Black Pepper

Before cleaning with sage smudge or incense, burn black pepper to get rid of bad energies in your home.

Catnip

Catnip was heavily used in Medieval times for cooking and herbal medicines. Known for its calming effect on felines and humans, catnip is a great herb to use for incense. It produces a faint mint aroma which is refreshing and not overpowering. Burn to attract a new love or relationship.

Cedar

A sacred plant to many cultures, cedar has been used both to purify and drive out negative energy, as well as bring in good influences. It is often burnt to bless a new house just as people are moving in.

Dill

One of the earliest uses of dill was as a soothing medicinal herb in ancient Egypt. The ancient Babylonians were also known to have cultivated dill. It's still widely used today and carries a fresh, light, herbaceous aroma. Add in workings to aid in romantic love, everyday protection, and money.

Dragon's Blood

Dragon's Blood resin comes from several species of palm tree. When cut, the roots and tree "bleed" a deep red resin, which has been used as a holy incense, dye, and varnish for centuries. The reason it is sometimes called "Dragon's Blood Reed" is that the resin used to be packaged for export in palm reed leaves.

Dragon's Blood resin is often used as a substitute for human or animal blood when working with antiquated incense or spell recipes. Dragon's Blood is great for almost any magickal purpose: from love to hexing, power to protection. The resin will add power to any working. Burned alone, Dragon's Blood is cleansing and empowering.

Frankincense

Frankincense is the dried resin of an African tree. Once prized equally with myrrh and gold, it's used in meditation and healing. This herb has a long history, especially known for cleansing and protecting the soul. I have heard of it being used to help ease the transition into death when it's necessary for someone to let go.

High John the Conqueror Root
High John the Conqueror is an indomitable figure of American folklore: He is said to have been an African Prince, enslaved in the south, but liberated by his own guile and will. He is never said to have had his spirit broken, therefore retained the will to trick his "master" into freeing him.

After freeing himself, High John is said to have returned to Africa, but left his spirit and power in the High John Root, that he may continue to care for his people until his return. It is said that merely by speaking the name of High John the Conqueror, one may invoke his power and protection.

The root itself is a boon to any working – the root readily accepts and amplifies any magickal charge and is used for almost every magickal purpose under the Sun or Moon. Though they are most commonly used as an ingredient in mojo bags, High John Roots can just as easily be buried, placed in locations of import, or carried alone on the person. For nearly any purpose, anoint a High John the Conqueror Root with the appropriate oil for the working, combine with an odd number of herbs, and a single stone. This root can be used as a talisman in any working: health, wealth, love, courage, luck – you name it!

Hyssop
The name 'hyssop' stems from the Greek word 'hyssopos' and the Hebrew word for 'esov', meaning 'holy herb'. Hyssop's aroma is a great pick-me-up, some even claim it smells like licorice. Its aroma can also be described as fruity, woody and slightly sweet.

Juniper
The branches of this evergreen were once used for temple purification

rituals. Juniper is especially helpful to invigorate your mind and body when tired. It was also burned during the plague to resist illness.

Lavender

Lavender's history dates back approximately 2,500 years and is believed to have originated in the Middle East, Mediterranean and India. There's no mistaking the peaceful aroma of lavender. The dried flower buds of lavender have a light refreshing scent when burned. They're often incorporated into ceremonies that are focused on peace, restful sleep, and happiness. Lavender can be burned therapeutically to address insomnia, depression, grief, sorrow, and anxiety.

Marjoram

The ancient Greeks greatly valued marjoram, using it as a natural remedy for many ailments. Marjoram possesses a mild, sweet aroma with woody notes. Ideal for adding refreshing vibes to your living space. This plant is used to clean and dispel negativity.

Mugwort

Perhaps the most famous of magickal herbs in modern times as a symbol of witchcraft, surpassing even the infamous Mandrake. Mugwort's dried leaves are used to cleanse space of negative energies. When burned before bedtime, it's known to stimulate dreams. This herb is used for a range of purposes, including love, healing, protection, prophecy, and dreams. The fumes of Mugwort are also an excellent offering to her patron goddess and namesake Artemis.

Myrrh

Myrrh is another valuable resin, which comes from a nearly leafless Middle Eastern shrub. Ancient Egyptians used it for healing and to embalm bodies. It is currently used for meditation, spirituality, happiness, transformation, strength, confidence, and stability.

Patchouli

Patchouli is traditionally used for attraction. Because of its warm, rich scent, it is believed to attract love, lust, or success: things of the Earth. In modern practice, especially in the Hoodoo and Conjure practices of the American South, Patchouli is used in both positive and negative lights: for cursing, separation, and bane – as well as love and money.

Peppermint

Peppermint was originally cultivated in England in the late seventeenth century. Its aroma can be described as cool and minty-fresh. Many have found its scent to enhance relaxation and concentration.

Peppermint is said to be a fine ingredient to include in any incense designed to increase prophetic dreams or psychic abilities. Peppermint can also be used for healing and cleansing: brew it into a tea and add to your bathwater to dispel evil or negative energy.

Rose

Who knew people burn dried rose petals for incense? In this form, this beautiful flower retains its abilities with attracting love and enhancing a romantic environment. It is also used for meditation and encouraging peace.

Rose Buds -Pink

Rose flowers are the most famous and popular herb for love spells. The Rose is beautiful, has an alluring aroma, and can easily draw blood with its sharp thorns. The fear of pain does not stop us from reaching for the Rose. Sound Familiar? Pink Rose Buds are added to love drawing incenses and mojo bags. You can also scatter Pink Rose buds on your altar when casting love spells. Red Rose Petals are often used for lust and passion; Pink Rose Buds are used for friendship, or True Love.

Rosemary

Rosemary has long been viewed as a soothing herb that encourages a sense of peace. When burned, rosemary produces a crisp, woodsy aroma that's sweet at the same time. It also goes well with sage bundles.

Rue

Rue has been used for centuries for protection and hex breaking. It is one of the most powerful, most essential magickal herbs for protection. A ubiquitous Italian protection charm, the "Cimaruta", grants protection from all ills. "Cimaruta" translates to "Sprig of Rue". Rue is sacred to the Moon Goddess Diana: a patron goddess of many Old and New World Witches.

Rue burned alone or with other herbs will make a powerful uncrossing incense. A bit of Rue added to just about any love incense is beneficial: it can protect you from undesirable suitors.

Sandalwood

Sandalwood Chips are one of mankind's first sacred wood incenses. It is an all-purpose herb, used for all manner of workings – from love to curses, healings to bindings, sacred offerings to banishing. Burned alone, Sandalwood cleanses and blesses a place, creates an atmosphere of love, and establishes sanctity.

Sage

Quite possibly the best-known ceremonial smudge plant, sage used for meditation, cleansing and purification. Many people burn it throughout their homes after a fight or to cleanse the energy left behind by a negative person.

Ancient Romans referred to sage as a plant of salvation (relating to the word 'salvare', meaning 'save'). It's also been used in ancient medicines for its natural healing properties. Sage's scent can be described as earthy and herbaceous.

Sweetgrass

This plant was sacred to the Native Americans. It's often braided before it dries, which is how you will find it for purchase. Sweetgrass has a light, sweet scent when burnt and is often used in conjunction with sage. After sage has chased out bad energy, sweetgrass attracts positive energy into the space. It is good for cleansing sacred space and is burned by many during prayers.

Thyme

The ancient Greeks and Romans purified their temples by burning bundles of thyme. It was believed that those who inhaled the incense received a boost of courage. Thyme is great for those wanting a more penetrating, invigorating aroma. Its scent can be described as both spicy and warming.

Part 6

MAGICKAL TEA & INCENSE RECIPES

Use the tea and incense together to create a magickal mindful moment. Or use them separately, tweak them to your likening, add your own special "something-something". Ultimately this is your magick to create.

May your teapot always be warm, and good cheer fill your home.

1.

A Magickal Awakening

It matters not the family born into or the land born upon, but your Spirit. If your spirit is Witchy, then you are Witchy. Drink this whenever you want to stir up some of your magickal energy. This tea is energizing, spicy, and digs down into your personal space to rumble that important part of you that both connects with the energy of the Earth, and Divinity at once.

An especially important herb for magickal power is Gingko Biloba. It is connected to the deepest, oldest magick and increases blood flow to body, allowing us to connect to that magick too. This is a recipe that connects, purifies, and protects you to awake your magick.

Tea Recipe
1 tablespoon Black Tea
1 tablespoon Ginkgo Biloba
1 teaspoon Rosemary (dried)
1 Cinnamon stick
1 cup hot water

Incense Recipe
1 teaspoon Rosemary
¼ teaspoon Cinnamon
1 teaspoon Cedar

2.
A Spring Goddess

This tea is best enjoyed with a vase of fresh cut flowers (wild picked if possible). This infusion honors the spring Goddesses who are one with many names. Each herb calls to this maiden Divine energy and is helpful to our respiratory tract.

This tea will, literally, let you breathe in the energy of the Spring Goddess. Mullein, specifically, is included as an offering to Dziewanna, the Maiden Spring Goddess whose name means Mullein. May you dance with her feisty femininity under the Spring moon.

Tea Recipe

1 tablespoon Green Tea

1 tablespoon Clover (white, if possible)

1 teaspoon Mullein

1 teaspoon Plantain

1 ½ inch piece Ginger root

1 cup hot water

Incense Recipe

1 teaspoon Sandalwood

1 teaspoon Thyme

3.
Beautiful Me

This is a tea that needs to be drank on a regular basis and include the mantra "Beauty within, beauty without, beauty surround me." Speak it aloud several times when drinking.

All these herbs are designed to be nourishing to your skin and create beauty on the outside as well as the inside. For example, when we use Calendula, commonly known as Marigold, externally it is a lovely herb for healing and nourishing skin.

However, magickally, these are little sparks of warm light in a thunderstorm. They give you internal, magickal sparks of light, creating beauty and suppleness to all they touch. Similarly, Helichrysum creates a beautiful exterior while connecting your soul to all things deeply spiritual.

Tea Recipe

1 tablespoon Rooibos Tea
1 tablespoon Calendula
1 teaspoon Helichrysum
1 wedge fresh Lemon
1 cup hot water

Incense Recipe

1 teaspoon Basil
1 teaspoon Hyssop
½ teaspoon Myrrh

4.

Divine Feminine

Great to use in full moon ritual, or for private times of decision making. To add extra punch, use full moon blessed water. What I find is a great use for this infusion is for those times when I feel jagged and caught up in hierarchies, boxes, and masculine energy of our world. When all I want is to reconnect to that which is feminine.

This tea will dig deep and connect you to the ancient feminine side of Divinity, and also reach out to the modern female energy to connect you to the Divinity in your community of moon sisters.

Tea Recipe

1 tablespoon Lavender

1 teaspoon Lemon Balm

1 teaspoon Nettle

Pinch Panax Ginseng

1 cup hot water

Incense Recipe

1 teaspoon Lavender

1 teaspoon Rue

½ teaspoon Mugwort

5.
Chakra Balancing

To deepen this experience, surround yourself with the colors associated to the chakras: red, orange, yellow, green, blue, indigo, violet. This infusion focuses on nourishing the entire energetic chakra system. It will help open your chakras, to put yourself in strength and equilibrium, to meet the next challenge.

In this recipe, there is a specific herb selected to represent each chakra. I will include the chakra and the color to focus on as you add each herb. Invite that color into your energy as you add the associated herb.

Tea Recipe
7 equal parts:
Root: Ashwagandha (Red)
Sacral: Damiana (Orange)
Solar Plexus: Chamomile (Yellow)
Heart: Hawthorn Berries (Green)
Throat: Marshmallow Root or Slippery Elm (Blue)
Third Eye: Mugwort (Purple)
Crown: Lavender (Deep Purple/White/Crystal Rainbow)
1 cup hot water

Incense Recipe
1 teaspoon Basil
1 teaspoon Bay
½ teaspoon Dragon's Blood
½ teaspoon Peppermint

6.
Find My Lost Stuff

As you drink the tea imagine your object returning to you. Don't forget to be careful walking over thresholds or through doorways as that may cause you to forget what looking for. This is a working built into the infusion, itself. Take the time to sit down and gather your ingredients with intent on finding the lost item.

You will need a tag lock, either directly connecting your lost item to this finding working or through symbolism. So, if you lost an item of clothing, you may use a button, maybe it was one of the additional buttons that came with the dress. If you lost some money, you might think about a shiny penny, maybe the very penny that sat next to the money later lost.

Either way, clean your tag lock well and place it in your teapot before adding the herbs knowing its connection to your lost item. Make sure you can get the item hot and wet. Continue to make and drink infusion, as usual but with powerful intent towards finding that item. Don't you worry, you will find it!

Tea Recipe
Small safe item for representation: penny, button, bead
1 tablespoon Ginkgo Biloba
1 teaspoon Caraway Seeds
1 pinch powered Ginseng
½ inch raw Ginger root
1 cup hot water

Incense Recipe
1 teaspoon Juniper
1 teaspoon Patchouli

7.

Love Yourself

"If you can't love yourself, how the hell you gonna love somebody else."
Rupaul

This tea brings a softer, kinder, more compassionate view of yourself, and don't we all need that? This recipe is about connecting to a deeper part of yourself and bringing love to even those hidden parts where you feel shame. It is about connecting to the energy of the moon.

All the ingredients are about love and directing that energy inwards. It is fiery and contains multiple power packed herbs specifically to combat our own inner dialogue. This is the start to dismantle that negative voice inside us all. This is your tea. Drink it with intention.

Tea Recipe
1 tablespoon Hibiscus
½ teaspoon Ginger
1 stick Cinnamon
5-6 Hawthorn Berries
Pinch Rose petals
1 cup red wine

Incense Recipe
1 teaspoon Cedar
1 teaspoon Thyme
1 teaspoon Lavender

8.

A Psychic Tea

When the moon is Dark, and standing in the crossroads is a welcoming idea, time to sip on this tea to see what possibilities may lay ahead.

Excellent to drink when doing divination. It is excellent for any dreamwork too. Whether you want lucid dreams, or you are looking to divine for a specific reason, this is the drink for you.

Take this by the sip as it can be bitter (that is part of the magick). Do not sweeten.

Tea Recipe
1 teaspoon Cinnamon
1 teaspoon Rose Petals
1 teaspoon Yarrow
1 teaspoon Mugwort
1 cup hot water

Incense Recipe
1 teaspoon Dill
1 teaspoon Mugwort
½ teaspoon Myrrh

9.

Spring Psychic

This psychic tea is different. We are starting with a tablespoon of Yarrow, a Witch's and a warrior's herb. It specifically increases the psychic powers of a Witch and stanches any of our physical and/or mental wounds along the way. Then we go about nicely, adding such bright and vibrant spring psychic herbs. Be careful with the punch of wormwood at the end, you will taste it!

This is an infusion that reminds me of my moon sister Daena, it is so light, bright, and beautiful, but watch out, there is a powerful dark punch hiding right under the surface.

Enjoy all the spring psychic magick your energy can handle.

Tea Recipe

1 tablespoon Yarrow

1 teaspoon Dandelion leaves

1 teaspoon Lemon Grass

1 pinch Wormwood

1 cup hot water

Incense Recipe

1 teaspoon Rue

1 teaspoon Hyssop

1 teaspoon Catnip

10.

Spirit in the Head

When Divinity calls us, it is up to us to answer. Do this through honor, reverence, and respect in all your endeavors and you will be blessed.

This potion allows us to be available to a state of possession so that an energy can flow through you. This is a place where we let go of the ego, let go of the id, and let spirit flow.

We are doing something very special with this recipe, we use sacred numbers to guide us to the final destination of spirit in the head. 1,3,5, and 7 build to a crescendo in this concoction that lets us enter the realm of the crossroads.

Combine all ingredients in a mason jar and mix every day for a week.

Tea Recipe
7 Cardamon Pods
1 Cinnamon stick
3 whole Red Peppers dried
1 fifth clear Rum

Incense Recipe
1 teaspoon Frankincense
1 teaspoon Myrrh

11.

Ancestral Connections

This tea is best drunk when using or creating an ancestral altar or wanting to connect to graveyard spirits.

Don't forget to bring a little extra for an offering if visiting spiritually connected land.

Tea Recipe

1 tablespoon Plantain

1 Bay leaf

Pinch of Mugwort

1 cup hot water

Incense Recipe

1 teaspoon Mugwort

1 teaspoon Basil

12.
Break-up/End Relationship

Sometimes you just gotta say "Goodbye". This is not about pushing people out the door. This is about being about to say the wise words you need to when you end a relationship.

When we know we need to break up, often there is a great deal of energy and anger surrounding the situation. This gives you the confidence and the words to say goodbye. This tea is all about calming down, counting to ten, and having the quiet assurance to do what needs to be done.

Tea Recipe
1 tablespoon Chamomile
1 teaspoon Echinacea
1 teaspoon dried Elderberry
1 sprig fresh Mint
1 cup hot water

Incense Recipe
1 teaspoon High John Conqueror
1 teaspoon Peppermint

13.

Forget the Sh%t of the Day

Time to take a good cleansing bath/shower, turn off from the world, sip a nice herbal tea and say to yourself over and over; "some folks just ain't right in the head, and you can't fix stupid."

You know those days when everything is in your face and intense? This is the tea for you. We start with a base of green tea, mildly stimulating and nourishing. To this we add all our other lovely herbs. Calm your nerves without putting yourself to sleep.

Give yourself calm, peace, and endurance.

Tea Recipe

1 heaping tablespoon Green Tea

1 heaping tablespoon Passionflower

1 teaspoon Oat Straw

1 teaspoon Lavender

1 cup hot water

Incense Recipe

1 teaspoon Lavender

1 teaspoon Agrimony

1 teaspoon Angelica

14.

Hear My Voice

This is not the hear my voice that must scream its words. It is intentionally nonassertive. It brings up the sort of powerful voice that does not need to yell. The drinker of this tea knows their own power and claims their own voice.

Your voice becomes a bell in the wind that people cannot help but listen to for its clarity and beauty. In any working where your voice must be heard and admired, drink this for three days prior to call on the energy you require.

This is an especially auspicious recipe if your voice is needed for money or love.

Tea Recipe

1 tablespoon Oat Straw

1 teaspoon Clover red

1 teaspoon Mullein

1 sprig fresh Mint

1 wedge Lemon

1 cup hot water

Incense Recipe

3 crushed Bay leaves

1 teaspoon Thyme

½ teaspoon Dragon's Blood

15.

Purification

In planning a ritual, I often start with purification. It is my policy to get in the shower prior to ritual as an act of purification. Sometimes I put herbs in a pouch in my shower to add to this special moment.

Afterwards, a moment of reflection to calm yourself and complete the purification prior to embarking upon the rest of your getting ready routine. In that moment, drink this tea.

Finish it with a dollop of honey to bring the sweetness of the Goddess to your ritual.

Both Hyssop and Orris Root were favorites of Marie Laveau.

Tea Recipe
1 tablespoon Hyssop
Pinch Orris Root powder
1 sprig fresh Rosemary
1 teaspoon Honey
1 cup hot water
Note- Taren is known to add a splash of rum to this

Incense Recipe
1 teaspoon Cedar
1 teaspoon Rosemary

16.

Talisman Warding

This purely magickal sickness ward that is designed to protect you energetically. Let this infusion be an addition to your physical and spiritual protections. As you are putting this potion together, take a moment to add each element specifically, and with intention.

Creating a protective energy needs power. I like to envision an energetic bubble all around me that filters out any yucky from getting through. Then, when I sip on the tea, I imagine that all of that plant spirit energy is charging and energizing my auric bubble.

Tea Recipe

1 tablespoon White Willow Bark

1 teaspoon Feverfew

Pinch Goat's Rue powder

1 cup hot water

Incense Recipe

1 teaspoon Rue

1 teaspoon Juniper

1 teaspoon Basil

17.
Ultimate Stress Relief

This is a time in history we will not soon forget. It is a time of heartache and grief for many. It is a time of stress for all. Even if you have not been personally touched by pandemic, quarantine has taken its toll, especially upon the extroverts.

Where before you may have been a bunch of sharp edges, this recipe will bring you soft, magickal, sweetness. Let this simple combination bring you out of your quarantine doldrums or any other stressful situation.

Tea Recipe

1 tablespoon Saint John's Wort
1 teaspoon Lavender
1 teaspoon Meadowsweet
1 cup hot water

Incense Recipe

1 teaspoon Lavender
1 teaspoon Marjoram

18.

F$#k This Crap

I hope when you are at your height of frustration, you sit back in your chair, and sip this infusion. Adding Yarrow and mint to your wine will have you wondering why you didn't do it sooner.

All these herbs work together with the alcohol to create a magickally aloof perspective. Add a dollop of pansy happiness and now you have a fresh new perspective and letting go of the crap of the day, even if it is just for this moment.

Tea Recipe
1 tablespoon Yarrow
Sprig fresh Mint
1 Pansy flower
1 cup White Wine

Incense Recipe
2 teaspoon Patchouli

19.

Summer Refresher

When you have had it, and are exhausted physically, mentally, or magickally, this infusion will help you rejuvenate and refresh. You will be cooled and yet, filled, with buzzing magickal energy.

This is a tea best drunk cold. Make it the same way you would make a sun tea.

Gather the herbs in a mason jar, pour your hot water over them and let the herbs sit for 10-15 minutes. Strain the herbs and let the tea sit in the sun for a few hours. When you feel the energy is garnered, take the tea inside and refrigerate, or serve over ice.

Tea Recipe

2 tablespoon Hibiscus

1 teaspoon Lavender

1 teaspoon Clover red

Splash Lemon-Lime soda

1 cup hot water

Incense Recipe

1 teaspoon Rose petals

1 teaspoon Dill

20.

Summer Solstice

This is the time of the year when the days are at their very peak. The energy of the sun is at its strongest. Although the sun is at its peak, it is also the time when the wheel of the year turns to the dark half. It brings the radiant solar energy of the solar and yet calls to the darkness to come.

This recipe combines herbs of the season in a cooling sun tea. During the summer, and especially on the solstice it is appropriate to make this tea.

Put all of the herbs in a mason jar. Fill the jar with hot water and let sit in the sun for 10-15 minutes. Strain herbs, then let the tea sit in the sun for a couple more hours ('til feels energized). Serve cold over ice.

Tea Recipe

1 tablespoon Saint John's Wort

1 teaspoon Chamomile

1 teaspoon Lavender

1 teaspoon Lemon Verbena

1 cup hot water

Incense Recipe

1 teaspoon Rosmary

1 teaspoon Sage

½ teaspoon Sandalwood

Part 7
FIVE GODDESSES OF THE WITCHES MAGICKAL TEA & INCENSE RECIPES

Inanna

Inanna is old and powerful. This Mesopotamian Goddess was worshipped in Sumer by the Acadians and the Babylonians, alike. The Nutmeg and Hyssop are ancient and hearken us back to a place and time not our own. Hyssop, especially, brings us to ritual and purification.

Like all our Goddesses, Inanna has many stories. In her descent to the underworld, She is required to remove all the regalia that makes Her the Queen of Heaven. One of the things that She must remove is Her Lapis Lazuli necklace.
Remind yourself of this story as you drop the blueberries in your tea, one by one and let yourself descend with Inanna.

Tea Recipe
1 tablespoon Hyssop
1 teaspoon Caraway Seeds
1 teaspoon dried blueberries
1 pinch ground Nutmeg
1 cup hot water

Incense Recipe
1 teaspoon Basil
1 teaspoon Hyssop
1 teaspoon Frankincense
½ teaspoon Lavender

Hecate

Every ingredient hearkens to this dark Goddess. Hecate loved herbs and had Her own garden. Some of Her favorite herbs were Mugwort, Mullein, and Mint. Yet, She grew and knew the spirits of many other plants.

For example, in the story of the Minotaur of Crete, She fed Dandelion to Theseus for 30 days so that he had the strength to kill the Minotaur. We add Dandelion, here, for that strength. We add Lavender because it is traditionally used to invoke Hecate.

Putting all this together and creating this infusion is a true homage to this Goddess of the Witchcraft of the Crossroads.

Tea Recipe

1 tablespoon Mugwort

1 teaspoon Dandelion

1 teaspoon Lavender

1 teaspoon Mullein

1 Sprig fresh mint

1 cup hot water

Incense Recipe

1 teaspoon Myrrh

1 teaspoon Sandalwood

Diana

Here we find our infusion dedicated to the virginal Goddess of wildlife and hunt. Apples are included because it is traditional to eat them at her feast day on August 13th. The apple is said to be the food of the Immortals and when cut crossways a pentagram is exposed directing us, ever further to the Goddess.

Both Lemons and Lemon balm are sacred to Diana.

Lemon balm draws things you desire to you, like the power of Diana. Drink this tea, connect to the moon and prophesy with the Mugwort, and let visions of Diana fill your mind.

Tea Recipe
1 tablespoon Lemon Balm
3-5 pieces dried Apple
2 fresh Lemon quarters
1 pinch Mugwort
1 cup hot water

Incense Recipe
1 teaspoon Mugwort
1 teaspoon Rue

Cerridwen

Cerridwen, called White Sow, is both Mother and Crone. Her stories are those of transformation, shapeshifting, and rebirth. In one story Her plans to make Her son wise and well-spoken are thwarted by Gwion Bach, Her assistant. After a year of stirring the mixture, he inadvertently tastes it, making it poison to anyone else. Cerridwen takes chase in Her anger. Gwion Bach shape shifts into all sorts of animals, and finally lands on a piece of grain. Cerridwen turns into a hen and snip snap She eats the grain boy whole.

Oat straw is the main constituent in this tea, both as nourishment for the soul, and as a nod to Her final victory in the chase. We include the Willow and the Yarrow to honor Her title as Lady of the Lake.

Here, She arises from the underworld, through the lake with Her cauldron allowing fallen soldiers to enter and be reborn. While you sip your Cerridwen infusion allow Her energy to wash over you, allowing you to shapeshift and be reborn.

Tea Recipe
1 tablespoon Oat Straw
1 teaspoon White Willow Bark
1 teaspoon Yarrow
2-3 pieces of Sow Thistle
1 cup hot water

Incense Recipe
1 teaspoon Sage
1 teaspoon Patchouli

Aradia

This is a dark Goddess that most people don't know very well. Her stories are not familiar to us yet and they need to be searched for and sought after. In fact, this beautiful bright Goddess's stories are still evolving and being created.

She invites you in to have your own experience and to create your own story. This mythical daughter of Diana and Lucifer is often called upon as the Queen of the Witches for love and sex magick. This is where this tea resides, in that Crossroads of Witchcraft, the unknown, and sex and procreation.

Drink it as a tonic to strength and refine the Aradia within you.

Tea Recipe

1 tablespoon Damiana

1 heaping teaspoon Red Clover

1 teaspoon Lemon Verbena

1 teaspoon Nettle

1 cup hot water

Incense Recipe

1 teaspoon Angelica

1 teaspoon Basil

1 teaspoon Cedar

Thank you so much for your support!

houseofwitchcraft.com

Please check out my other books available now

Hoodoo in the Palms
A Witch's Guide to the Season of the Dead
Bag Yo' Mojo
Crossroads Witchcraft; The Ingredients
Dedicant's Handbook to Coven Life

Coming Fall 2023

Conjuring Dirt; Magick of Footprints, Crossroads & Graveyards

ABOUT THE AUTHOR

Taren S

Southern conjuring Witch with over four decades of experience in the magickal community and a lover of high tea. To find out more please go to houseofwitchcraft.com